Written by: Karlene Rickard
Cover Design: Mike Hosannah
Illustrations: Earla Sylvester
Layout: Michael Williams for BIS Publications

First Printed September 2006
First Edition September 2006
Published by PMEC
www.pmec.org.uk, pmec2004@hotmail.com

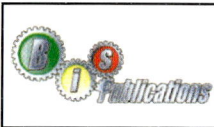

Support by BIS Publications
www.bispublications.com

New ISBN: 978-1-903289-09-9
Old ISBN:1-903289092

A catalogue record for this book is available from the British Library.

Dedication

To my son, Pianki Assegai to be used in his role as a parent, mentor, role model and teacher.

To those individuals who desire to nurture and shape young minds enabling them to become confident, responsible and well-being citizens.

Acknowledgments

Firstly, I would like to acknowledge God for inspiring me to record the many invaluable lessons taught to me by my son Pianki. This book represents the culmination of strategies developed during my own parenting journey and insights from the many parents who have so generously shared their experiences with me.

Secondly, my parents, Mr and Mrs Rickard, for the support and love they gave me through my life's journey. My dad walked proudly next to me to keep me mobile and active when my body was contorted through illness.

To my sisters, Yvonne Davies and Joanne Rickard for our adventures and laughter and their support. I could always rely on Yvonne to ensure that I looked good.

To my grand-dad, Mr Swinton, and deceased grandma with whom I spent my early years, for being positive role models, protectors and friends. I often rode on grandpa's shoulder and swung in the yards of material that made up grandma's skirts.

To my dear friend, Candy who has encouraged and supported me as an editor. To Ankhara, a very special friend who kept the flame alight when my vision got cloudy and my spirit weakened.

Contents

Introduction

Parenting, according to Doctor James Dobson, an American child psychologist,'Is not for cowards.'

Parenting can be tiring and demanding, yet joyous and fulfilling. Often we discover how to meet the responsibilities and challenges along the way and there really is 'never a dull moment.'

Most parents are keen to discover parenting strategies for themselves yet there are some tried and tested tools that work effectively. There is no need to reinvent the wheel. Therefore these tools can be used alongside your own strategies.

At the height of frustration, when you are unable to think, and your emotions are at boiling point; just sit down for a moment, count up to ten, reach for this book and apply the strategies within.

My life changed when I became totally paralysed and my son, Pianki, was only one year old. There I was, prostrate, needing to be cared for whilst Pianki needed me to parent him. Trusted friends and my devoted family took on the responsibility of nurturing us. With improved health, I was able to become more active as a parent. We played and read together, often recording the sessions. It was a delight to watch his beaming face as he read those stories and listened to the tape over and over, keeping him amused for hours. It developed in him a love for books and language. Sharing our traditions and values reinforced his culture and sense of belonging and also helped him to have a positive self-image.

Later in his development, when I became much better and mobile again, I wrote and developed a parenting programme and attended parenting workshops which helped Pianki and me to develop a better relationship based on honesty and appreciation.

I am so blessed to be sharing these wonderful tools with my son and I am sure he will use them with his children, my grandchildren.

Likewise, I hope you will find the information and tools in this book invaluable in establishing positive relationships with your children. Also, that your children develop into more confident, responsible and balanced individuals.

I have deliberately kept this book short so that parents can quickly and easily find key information. It is written in simple, parent friendly language so that it is easily accessible.

Thinking Stages and Age Appropriateness

Throughout this book I write about 'age appropriateness.' So it is important to clarify the phrase.

As children grow and develop from babies to adults, they experience the world in different ways. The developmental stages I describe here give you a general guide to children's phases of intellectual and emotional maturity at different ages in their lives. Of course, there will be some overlap between these development stages, each child develops in their own way.

Understanding these developmental stages can help us to think about our children more objectively and fairly as well as to create an environment conducive to healthy physical, emotional and social growth.

Babies are self-centred and rely on their physical senses to give them information about the world. Words used repeatedly by toddlers are 'me', 'mine', and 'my'. In fact, until children are about four years old, they can only see things from their own point of view. These young children need to be repeatedly told how to behave because they cannot easily remember a sense of 'right or wrong' behaviour. We have to constantly reinforce the correct ways to behave, even though we may feel that we have repeated it a hundred times.

After this early development stage, between five and eleven years, children start to respond to those in authority and can understand more about what they can do. There is a tendency for children of this age group to start to negotiate their rights, seeing themselves as equal to those that are older, including their parents. In fact, it is around this age that children are more likely to do tasks if they can see how they would benefit. They are concerned that everything is 'fair' as it relates to them.

Young people between 12 to 16 years of age think a lot about their image. To them, it is very important to be accepted by their friends, so the influence of peers can be more powerful than other sources of influence. That is why it is important by this stage to have established clear boundaries, age appropriate responsibilities and to have developed a positive relationship with your child that has been built on trust, open communication and understanding. This will help them to develop independence in their thinking, and to withstand some of the negative peer pressure.

Young adults over sixteen become more aware of their position, rights and responsibilities within society. Hence, it is necessary, difficult as it seems, to allow them to make their own choices and decisions.

The above development stages progress in a spiral fashion. Often a child will return to an earlier stage of emotional and physical behaviour for a while, for example when a new baby comes into the family. Though normal, this must be monitored and if you have major concerns you need to seek support by talking to your child's teacher, a doctor or an elder in the community.

In assessing age appropriateness for responsibilities. These factors need to be taken into consideration:

- . The actual age and physical development of the child i.e. your child is physically or intellectually able to carry out tasks with minimum supervision.

- . The safety of the child. Has the child's thinking developed enough to understand what is required without causing danger to herself and others?

- . Positive modelling. Has the child been given clear instructions and been supervised carefully?

Appreciation

Children's greatest desire is to have the attention and appreciation of their parents. Therefore, It is important to observe something different that our children does every day. We need to have fun with them.

We must praise our children for positive attitudes, behaviour, effort or achievement. Most importantly, we must praise our children for just being who they are. Very soon they will be praising us.

We can ignore some of the less severe, unwanted behaviours such as always trying to seek our attention. Eventually, they will stop unnecessary attention- seeking behaviour. Of course, if our children are putting themselves, others or properties at risk, we need to deal with the situation immediately.

What to do:

Praise your child daily.

Move close to your child.

Look directly at your child.

Call your child by name.

Look pleased.

Say to your child exactly what you have heard them saying or observed them doing and demonstrate your appreciation through praise. Be specific, for example, "I really like the way you style your hair."

Say to your child why you appreciate them or how you feel about them such as, "I am blessed to have you as my son" or "I enjoy listening to you; you are very knowledgeable for one so young."

Show your child physical affection; you could give him a hug or just a gentle touch.

Give new responsibilities to encourage the continued development of the observed qualities, for example, letting your child style your hair.

Praise your child publicly in front of other members of the family or to friends, provided you are sure they will be comfortable with this.

Look for appropriate behaviour to praise. In praising your child for appropriate behaviour, you are building an account of trust and good relationships that you can draw on when things are not going too well.

Beliefs

There are many ways of regarding human spirituality. For some people, spirituality is closely associated with a religious belief, for others it is not. Some regard spirituality as the ultimate state of being to which they can aspire as humans. For others, it has to do with acknowledging the greatness of nature and the wonders of the world. A spiritually focussed person can be said to be someone who stands in awe of what is not understood. It can also be recognition of the interrelatedness of everything on the planet. Some people associate it with something they call the supernatural.

Our spiritual development plays a critical part in our becoming balanced and stable individuals. Although our spiritual dimension is not measurable, it is an essential part of our lives. Our spiritual well being is associated with our beliefs. Therefore, we need to share our spirituality, our beliefs and faith with our children when they are young so that they can develop their own beliefs.

When they become teenagers, and if negative peer pressure starts to impact on their lives, they will be in a much better position to resist If their spiritual beliefs are strong. If their beliefs and spiritual foundation are weak, they will be more easily influenced by others.

What to do:

Talk to your child about:

. Your beliefs, For example, "I believe that we were created by God and he has made all of us unique and special with a specific purpose to be fulfiled in our lives."

. The three dimensional make-up of human beings - The three elements being soul, body and spirit. They work together to create harmony.

. The importance of having a time of reflection.

. The importance of trusting in God (if you believe in God).

. Some of the spiritual or supernatural experiences you have had. For example, "I was afraid to take part in the school play but once I believed that everything would be okay and everyone was doing their best, things went very well."

. Some of the fears and challenges you have faced and how you were able to overcome them.

. Some of their own spiritual experiences and beliefs.

Demonstrate ways in which your beliefs are practiced, such as giving to charity, or modelling how you pray.

If you normally have devotional times, on occasions, encourage your child to be actively involved by leading the sharing, reading or singing.

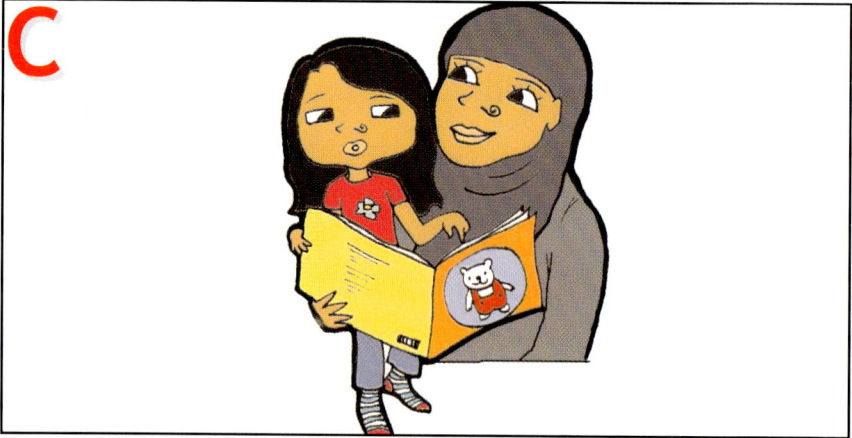

Communication

We need to be able to communicate effectively in order to live a balanced and healthy life. This can be verbal or non verbal.

Children become aware that everyone, including themselves, has the right to be heard and respected. Therefore we have to be sensitive and caring when communicating whilst ensuring that our own views are made clear.

We can put communication styles into three groups:

Aggressive communication
This is where our main concern is that our own thoughts, ideas and opinions are heard and accepted. Views are expressed in a hostile and insensitive manner without regard for the other person's opinion and feelings.

Passive communication
This is where we fail to express our true thoughts and feelings, or express them without conviction. We give away our rights to others and allow them to dismiss our suggestions and opinions.

Assertive communication
This is where our main concern is that our own thoughts, ideas and opinions as well as the person we are communicating with, are expressed openly and honestly.

5

What to do:

Discuss the three styles of communication with your child. You could role-play the different styles to give a clear feel of what they are like.

Talk with your child about:

. The feelings that result when we experience the different communication styles and ask your child to share occasions when they may have experienced the different styles.

. The communication styles that they have experienced in their day to day life.

. What is likely to happen when different communication styles are used.

Get your child to practice the different kinds of communication styles.

Emphasize that the best way to communicate is when one is being assertive, listening carefully, putting one's point of view forward in a strong, but sensitive manner such as, "I can see why you might be anxious about this, given what happened before. However, this situation is not the same. I have learned from the previous experience and this will help me to grow and develop"

Identify times when negative communication has taken place in the home, outside, in school or at church. Talk about what may have caused them to be negative and look at what could have made it positive.

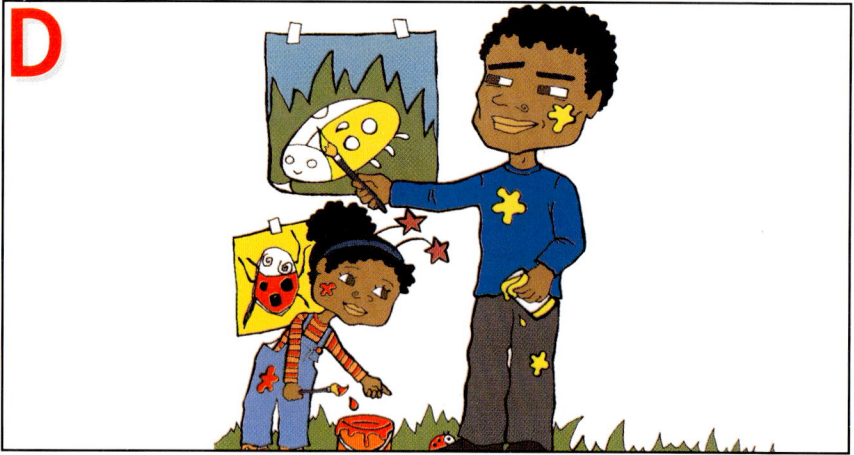

Discovering Together

Life is a learning process from the cradle to the grave. No one person can reach a point of saturation in all areas of learning. Nevertheless, we often behave as if we are the font of all knowledge because we don't want our children to think less of us.

But of course, we are only human and can make mistakes like everyone else. Our children need to see us making mistakes and solving problems so that we can model how to deal with challenges.Therefore, we need to establish a firm, honest, stable environment for learning together.

When our children are given the opportunity to teach us, their confidence will develop and we will learn more about each other, as well as understand each other's vulnerability.

My son teaches me how to use the computer and he often gets frustrated with me. This helps me understand some of the experiences we have when learning something new. It also provides an opportunity to talk about the challenges we both encounter and allows us to learn together.

A friend of mine, who is disabled, said her father treated her the same as her siblings. She grew up doing the same things as her brothers and sisters. This gave her tremendous confidence in her abilities.

What to do:

Show your child that you have strengths and weaknesses and that it is important to be honest about what you can and cannot do. This will enable them to become confident and competent individuals.

Show your child that you are as vulnerable to mistakes as they are, and that you are prepared to learn from your mistakes. This will encourage open and honest communication between yourselves. Of course, showing your child your vulnerability does not mean you will allow them to be rude or disrespectful. You will model respect towards them and expect them to show you respect in return.

Your child will think more of you if you are honest. If you acknowledge when you are wrong and strive to learn and improve, they will too. You are modelling effective behaviour.

Read together as often as possible. Teenagers could be invited to read the newspapers with you and discuss some of the issues.

Encourage your child to teach you something new everyday and tell them that you learnt it from them.

Play different games together.

Watch video and television programmes and discuss them.

If you have a young or a disabled child you could:

- Get a scrapbook and save pictures or 'momentos'.

- Collect labels and create posters of your favourite foods.

- Create simple recipes together.

E

Ethnicity

Ethnicity is one's racial and cultural heritage. It is what gives each group a sense of being different.

Children can feel lost if they don't know anything about their family ancestry and cultural background. We need to help children to map out and to appreciate their heritage. This will help them to develop their own sense of worth, self-esteem as well as teaching them how to love themselves and their culture.

As parents and carers, we should not allow these unique, cultural traditions to be lost between generations, and thus creating a generation gap.

If we don't share our cultural roots with our children, we are at risk of creating a distance between our children and ourselves which, at a later stage, can develop into disrespect and self-hate.

What to do:

Practice cultural rites of passage (passing from one stage of development to another) such as the celebration of adolescence.

Acknowledge and celebrate your child's transitions and explain to your child how proud you are of their growth and achievements.

Attend cultural events and celebrations with your child.

It would be wonderful if you could take your child to visit your country, district, or place of origin.

Bridge the generational gap by visiting grandparents, or elders of the same culture, if your parents are no longer around.

Share books and encourage reading that relates to your culture, especially where your culture is not often represented in the books and films of the larger community.

Together, Research information about your background or ancestors and discuss this with your child.

Acknowledge and celebrate the achievements of heroes and heroines from your cultural background.

F

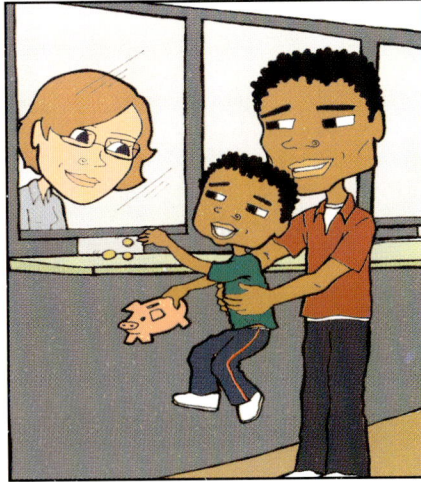

Financial Literacy

It is very easy to become a great consumer instead of investing and developing business in our highly materialistic culture. As parents, we need to be clear about what we model in terms of consuming and producing. Communities and racial groups who predominantly consume, can become economically impoverished. This could result in them being dependent on others to provide employment and windows of opportunity for themselves and their children. Some of us allow our money to manage us rather than the other way around.

Our children need to know how to spend, save and invest money. They need to be educated into effective money management so that in later life they will become financially independent.

It is important to start teaching our children about money from an early age. Three years is not too young. I introduced to some parents with children under five the practice of getting them to save one or two pence weekly. After five weeks, the parents with their children counted out five pennies and then exchanged the pennies for a five pence coin. After a few weeks, one parent reported that her five year old son asked to use some of his savings to buy a card for her.

What to do:

Help your child to become financially literate by encouraging them to save and use their own money for a range of purposes.

Show your child how to invest money in a savings account, for example, and see it grow.

Discuss different ways of saving and work out the most effective ways that are suitable to them.

Give your child pocket money. Teach them how to budget.

Take your child shopping for the family groceries and share information about the cost of purchases you need to make.

Share aspects of your income and expenditure for bills and costs with your child and how you work out your budget.

Discuss the importance of making certain purchases by explaining how to compare the price, type and quality of different items.

Play cards and educational board games, for example, Scrabble and Monopoly, in order to develop their monetary vocabulary, strategic planning and their skills such as handling money.

Help your child to create honest ways of generating money and resources for example car cleaning, gardening etc.

Teach your child to give to charity and to pay dues or tithes (one tenth of one's income paid to charity or the church).

G

Gender

Gender is a sociological term used to refer to maleness or femaleness. In the western world, boys are often given less responsibilities and more freedom. This shapes their commitment and responsibility in adulthood.

To make sure our sons and daughters become responsible, sensitive and caring adults, we have to nurture them appropriately from an early age. It is very important that we teach both our sons and daughters the full range of skills required for happy, successful independent living, to ensure we raise men and women who are capable, sensitive and caring.

Just to reflect. Is your daughter angry because she finds herself doing the chores around the house whilst your son plays with his play station? Is your son angry because he always has to wash the car?

Responsibilities must be given according to a child's developmental age, not according to their gender.

We should always praise both our sons and daughters according to their response to the family rules and for being special to us.

What to do:

Teach your sons and daughters how to clean or cook beginning with very simple meals. At a young age (six to seven years old) properly supervised children can set the table, prepare a cold breakfast, help to wash the salad and make a cold drink.

Between the ages of ten and twelve (depending on maturity) mentor your child to prepare a simple family meal at least once a month. In some cultures it can be earlier.

Involve children in the following types of chores:

> · Shopping for basic food items
> · Washing dishes and clothing
> · Gardening, raking, sweeping and planting
> · Cleaning the car

Older children, i.e. those over nine years old can be taught how to cook using gas and electricity but they must be supervised at all times.

Special time (time when you allow your son or daughter to have personal time or time to help in caring for grandparents, brothers and sisters) should be given separately and equally.

Affection should be shown equally to both sons and daughters privately and publicly. Be aware of their developmental stages. There is an age when your child will not appreciate public demonstration of your affection.

H

Healthy Life Style

To live a healthy life we need to be balanced spiritually, mentally, physically and emotionally. This means taking care of our mental and physical health as well as being able to manage our feelings and develop our spirituality. We need to know how to have fun with ourselves and how to share special moments with our children.

It has been stated by various psychologists, that more young people in the twenty first century are becoming academically accomplished but emotionally unstable and spiritually unaware.

It is important for us to help our children to achieve a life of balance so that they can grow and develop healthily.

What to do:

Arrange to spend consistent and regular time weekly with each child. If you are unable to keep that agreed time, apologise to your child and reschedule. Remember, your child deserves the same respect you give to your employer. In fact, work is important but family is essential.

Arrange to spend regular time with your friends and your spouse to ensure that you maintain adult contact and continue to develop your personal interests whilst you raise your children. You will be a better parent when you maintain the right balance of relationships and activities. Remember, your whole life is not centred around being a parent.

Encourage your child to talk very openly and honestly about their feelings. Model this by talking about your own feelings in a calm and loving way, even when you are feeling upset.

Games are also a way to help children handle winning, losing, jealousy and disappointment and to talk about the feelings involved.

Talk about food, nutrition, good hygiene and exercise and their effects on the body. Plan meals, and exercise together and help your children to understand the importance of a healthy diet. You should model healthy eating.

peter's 1st concert

Island of Competence

Our children have gifts and talents which are like their own special islands over which they have the potential to master. We need to recognise and encourage the development of their gifts from an early age. These gifts might include, for example, their ability to organise, negotiate, or to write. A parent told me that her son at aged five used to get up early and write stories. She was often annoyed with him for waking her up so early which resulted in him becoming frustrated, angry and loosing interest in writing. Even the illustrator of this book loved to draw from the age of three and yet again her mother would get very angry and she wanted her to read books instead. Today she looks at her daughter's beautiful work and feels guilty.

We should not wait for others, such as school teachers, to tell us what to nurture in our children. Instead, let's try to catch the emergence of those new skills, talents and gifts in our children and bring them alive by praising, encouraging and providing opportunities to develop them.

As a challenge let us ask ourselves whether we know our children's true interests and abilities. If not, how can we find out?

What to do:

Help your child to recognise his or her natural gifts and abilities.

When you observe a new quality in your child you can bring it to life by acknowledging, celebrating and helping it to develop. Your children may be creating music with the pots and pans!

Create a 'Personal Island of Gifts and Talents' with your child as follows:

. Explain to your child that together you are going to chart some of the special qualities and passions which you have observed, plus those they share with you.

. Together, draw the outline of a Talent Map on a sheet of A4 paper. It can be the child's own design, for example, a map of a country he or she likes.

. Over the next four weeks, for each talent put a coloured star on the Talent Map. You can also get your child to write on the map the talent you noticed or stick on a coloured star and write the achievement on it.

· At the end of four weeks, talk about the talents and gifts your child has shown. Ask your child if they would like to add to the list and chart. Celebrate their achievement and decide what should be done to develop one or two of the new talents.

J

Justice

It is so important to ensure that each developmental stage in our children's lives is acknowledged, worked through appropriately and celebrated. This is known as the **rite** of passage. Our children deserve the **right** to make a safe transition from one stage to the next.

Before we know it, they are out of nappies and leaving home to meet the challenges in the world. We must do our best to prepare them for the journey ahead.

We must establish age appropriate rules and responsibilities to take our children to their next level of physical, spiritual, emotional and intellectual development. Remember, it is our children's **right** to be given responsibilities.

What to do:

Ensure that you use age appropriate language and behaviour with your children.

Make sure you are fair when setting rules by:

- Knowing the developmental stages, and work within their remit

- Ensuring that Safety and non-negotiable issues are enforced with explanations

- Treating each child according to their stage, of development

With a younger child, be sure to constantly reinforce what you expect and need them to do.

Be willing to negotiate certain rules and activities with an older child and give appropriate responsibilities to develop their skills further, for example, getting home on time and preparing the table for family dinner.

Moving from one school to another or from one year group to another is an important rite of passage and needs to be prepared for and celebrated. Talk with your child about any anxieties they might have about going to secondary school and help them to allay their fears by developing strategies with them.

Honour what was negotiated, financial and otherwise, even if your child does something else that upsets you. If this is the case, discuss the behaviour you are concerned about and work on an appropriate consequence for unacceptable behaviour.

Celebrate the journey into adolescence for boys and girls. The beginning of menstruation for girls needs to be seen as positive. For example, mother and daughter could go away for the weekend to celebrate and discuss the changes. Father and son could go away to mark the journey into the teenage years.

K

Keys for boundaries

We all need boundaries. When our children come into the world, everything is unfamiliar to them, even being surrounded by the air we breathe. It is our responsibility to help them to make sense of the world. In helping them we are teaching acceptable behaviour, habits, values and norms such as listening to others and washing hands before eating.

It is important that rules are established and, boundaries are understood. We must always check the rules with our children by asking them to repeat what is expected of them. It is not good enough to accept a "yes" response. Their understanding could be a misunderstanding.

When our children fail to respond as agreed, then we should respectfully go through the consequences. Consequences could be logical or natural. Logical consequences are situations determined by the person in authority. For example, if a teen breaks curfew, they are not allowed out the next night. Natural consequences are situations that are not controlled by anyone, they happen naturally. If you put your finger in an electric socket, you get a shock.

We must remember that rules without a healthy relationship lead to rebellion.

What to do:

Make sure your child understands the importance of having boundaries and rules to avoid natural consequences, for example, running could result in a serious injury.

Rules are needed to help your child to develop appropriately and for the world to be safe and for people to work effectively together

From an early age set a pattern for:

Sleeping - your child needs enough sleep even if he or she does not want to. You must be firm and consistent.

Eating - we are what we eat. Your child needs to have a balanced diet as relates to their developmental stage. Eat more vegetables and fruits instead of artificially flavoured foods such as crisps and chocolate. Your child's taste buds will learn to accept what is healthy once you train them.

Activities - a range of physical and mental activities are important to develop their muscles and get their systems to function correctly, for example developing eye/hand coordination. Activities might include hop scotch, chess, brisk walking, kicking balls, throwing and catching.

Socialising - it is important to know who your child's friends are. They should be welcomed to your home and there should be clear rules or agreements about times and places for being out socialising or playing. It would be inappropriate for a thirteen year old to be out after 10 p.m. without adult supervision.

L

Listening

Listening is one of the most constructive tools we have. It involves the whole body, looking at the person and observing their actions and expressions. Listening skills need a lot of practice. When we only listen in part we can miss some important details and are likely to respond inappropriately and ineffectively to the situation. This can result in negative conflict because the child feels unheard, under-valued and unloved.

When the whole body is engaged in listening, we develop active listening skills, which means hearing the words, empathising with the feeling, nodding and encouraging the person to speak. Active listening does not mean you should not follow through with the consequence if the child has broken a rule or shown disrespect.

In listening, it is important to separate facts from feelings and opinions.

What to do:

Model good listening skills in order to help your child to develop the same: Remove yourself from distractions and say, "I'm listening to you". Concentrate on what your child is saying.

Use good eye contact and touch if necessary. Listen for what is being said.

Use verbal cues where necessary, for example nodding, smiling and saying "uhmms". Listen for feelings. Carefully observe body language such as facial expressions, hand gestures or movements of the feet etc. There may be more information in what your child is doing with their body than what they are saying.

Articulate your observations about their body language for example, "I notice you squeeze your hands together every time you say ...."

Check if you are hearing correctly what's being said by paraphrasing what you believe your child has said. Listen for repeated phrases, thoughts and feelings.

Listen with a balanced approach to help the child to clarify what the real issues are.

You need to:

- · Ask questions, or say out loud what you think is happening. keep this up until you get to the real facts and your child feels understood.

- · Keep the facts separate from your feelings.

- · Avoid reacting to phrases like 'Well all my friends can do ....' or It is not fair.'

If you are angry, be sure to pause, breathe and centre yourself before speaking. Feelings of anxiety, anger, and pain can confuse the real issues and make them more difficult to understand.

Go into the countryside, the park or a field with your child just to listen to nature.

M

Modelling

Modelling is the first and most effective mode of teaching. If our children shout and we bellow, *'Speak quietly I am not deaf,'* we are modelling that it is fine to shout.

We may insist that they do their homework in a quiet room because a good education is important, yet the chances are, they will see us watching the television more often than they see us reading.

We get mad at our teenager for not washing up the plates, but for years when they were growing up, we allowed them to sit and watch television whilst we washed up. We have modelled to them that it is okay to let others do all the household chores.

In some small ways we often treat others and our parents unkindly yet we get upset if they are disrespectful to us and others.

We need to consistently speak quietly to our children in order to model right communication. When our children shout, we need to remain calm and refuse to respond to their shouting. Life is more caught than taught, so we need to be very careful about what we are modelling.

What to do:

Be as conscious about the things you do as the things you say. It is what you do which will most influence your child's behaviour and attitude.

Model the calm manner in which you would like your child to communicate with you.

Give special time to each child if you have more than one. This will demonstrate that they are loved and respected. If father spends special time with his daughter, she will develop a sense of what to expect from a partner when she is of age.

Show lots of affection to family members daily and they will do like wise.

Always say 'please and thank you' and give explanations for social rules and insist on them from your children. They will develop good social skills as a result.

Boys need to observe their fathers contributing to the running of the household in a range of ways not just seeing them carrying out DIY tasks. Boys and girls should be expected, and encouraged, to do housework, cooking, gardening and develop a range of survival skills to be able to live independently.

There are certain behaviours and attitudes that you can develop in your child by introducing them to books and films that portray good role models. For example, in the book 'Gifted Hands', Dr Ben Carson shared how he overcame some mental, social and racial barriers. He is a pioneer in medical science.

N

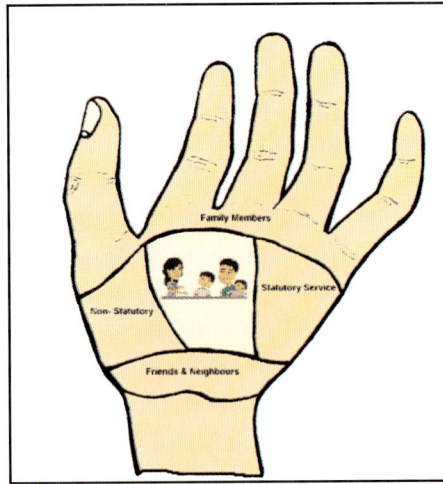

Network of Support (Hand of support)

We all need support in order to live and enjoy the gifts of life. The African proverb, **'It takes a village to raise a child,'** is very relevant to living a healthy life style.

In these times, modern villages do not necessarily need to be geographical locations but simply networks of families who support and rely on each other. The helping hand diagram above shows other families, friends, neighbours, official and non-statutory professionals that surround us. We need to be clear about who we can call on and for what. We also need to know who our children see as their sources of support. Traditionally in Africa, a child has many parents.

The skills of asking for and giving support are very important and we should model this to our children. This will help them to develop working relationships in the family and the community and to respect others in their environment. We should never ever feel ashamed of asking for help. Using a support network will give us freedom of mind, time and space and allow us to grow as a family.

What to do:

Talk to your child about your network of support and allow them to become a part of that support system.

Regularly talk with your child about their different resources for support.

Find out what and who is available to support you and your family, and share it with them. Use the diagram to explore how those around you can become your support network. Look at the four areas shown on the diagram: family, statutory and non-statutory agencies, professionals, friends and neighbours, and construct your hand of support as follows:

- Identify, discuss and list those who you would feel comfortable and safe to call upon for support

- Include your child's suggestions, at least one person in each area

- Make sure everyone in the family is involved in the process

- Display the list where your child can see it.

Surround your child with people who have the same values and can positively mentor them.

On Line for Development

It is important that we are fully aware of the developmental stage of our children, as different sets of tools and approaches are needed to raise and manage them at each stage. For example, between the ages of six to eleven our children tend to ask a lot of questions and want to negotiate everything. Therefore, we need to know how to confidently negotiate with them whilst maintaining boundaries. Refusing to negotiate at this stage would be ultimately damaging to them.

Negotiation is a key life skill which is essential in a range of work and personal relationships. We can use negotiation skills with our children in order to get them to do things they may not want to do. For example, you might want to negotiate a new homework timetable by saying, *"If you start your Mathematics homework now, I'll let you have some extra time to finish off that fantastic drawing you started. What would you like to do?"*

It is important for us to understand each stage of development so that we can use the most effective and appropriate approaches. The appropriate language, rules, responsibilities, incentives, consequences and rewards are all essential.

What to do:

0 -1 year
Provide lots of stimulation. This can include the following:
> ·Smiles, different expressions, colourful mobiles, cubes, bricks, soft toys, soft plastic objects when bathing, talking and singing whilst using baby's name and playing different types of music.

Provide routine. This can include the following:
> · Regular feeding , regular bathing and regular story times.

Provide familiarity
> · Talk a lot so that your child recognise your tone of voice within different situations
> · Copy your baby's sounds, watching and waiting until they respond, then continue the dialogue and include your baby in social gatherings.

2 to 3 years
> · Sensitively increase the challenge of activity you give to your child.
> · Give your child little jobs around the house(for example. putting their toys) in the toy box and celebrate new positive behaviour.
> · Explain things in the environment in very simple language.
> · Teach options for expressing feelings rather than hitting and biting.
> · Play with them and encourage your child to play cooperatively with other children.

4 to 6 years
> · Develop and reinforce rules and agreements in the home
> · Develop social behaviour, for example, how to behave when there are visitors.
> · Encourage sharing with other children and adults.
> · Expose the child to different social environments such as celebrations, worship and play activities.

P

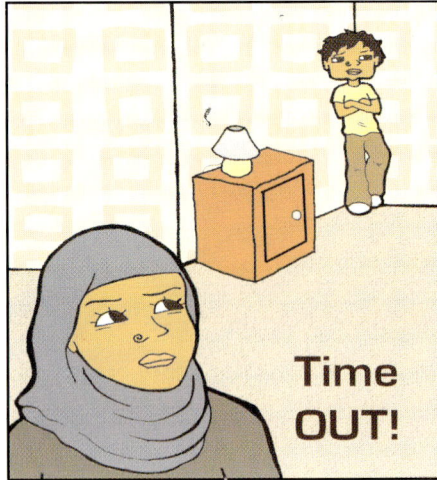

Physical Punishment

At times when our children persist with being disobedient and demonstrate unacceptable behaviour, our immediate reaction might be to give a quick, sharp smack. It might seem the best solution but as the behaviour is repeated, the smack can get harder and more premeditated. Where does a smack end and physical abuse begin?

Physical punishment models aggression. We need to model other strategies for our children or they may become aggressive and abusers of others, for example bullying siblings or other children at school.

Research on bullying and on children with some behaviour disorders has shown that physical punishment is often a contributing factor. We need to remember that the word discipline means to teach and not to punish.

What to do:

Teach your child how to behave appropriately

Get your child's attention.

Call your child by name and wait until they are looking at you. Describe what kind of behaviour you expect and why, using clear language.

Check for understanding by asking your child to explain the behaviour that is expected.

Invite a response from your child to find out if they are able to follow through.

Once you have agreed on the appropriate behaviour, determine the consequence. Older children can have a greater say in determining the logical consequences.

If you need to, be sure to immediately follow through with the consequence. Remain calm - taking deep breaths if you are angry.

Alternatives to physical punishment include the following:

- . Time out: this is a period away from others but within sight during which your child is able to reflect on their behaviour. One minute for each year of age is generally effective.

- · Removal of privileges: children can be denied the opportunity to take part in activities which are over and above everyday routines. This should never include normal meals.

- · Imposing sanctions: sanctions might include being grounded or being denied access to computer games or favourite television programme.

Quality Time

The quantity and quality of the time we spend with our children are both important. However, it is ultimately the quality of time that matters most. Limited quality time is much more effective, than a lot of time together without any positive interaction. We need to make our children know that they are special by giving them both quantity and quality time. We can ask ourselves the following questions when thinking about quality time:

> How often do we have special time with each child, doing activities such as walking for pleasure, reading and playing together?

> Is that quality time negotiated with our child and is it really quality time?

It is good to get into a routine whereby you have protected, regular time together. If you are unable to keep to the arranged time, remember to apologise, explain and reschedule. Quality time will provide the platform to develop a positive and healthy relationship.

What to do:

Secure a regular and a consistent time for each child when they can have your full attention, and you can simply enjoy just being together. In these spaces, it is important that you just listen to what your child has to say, if they want to talk, without you being critical or finding solutions for them.

Quality time does not have to be full of speaking and doing. Moments of silence by the river bank or in a hammock as you both read are perfectly valid.

How much time each child needs is a very individual matter, but generally speaking, under fours need a minimum of about 15 minutes each day and for older children, at least an hour a week. Teenagers need quality time too! Even in adulthood, quality time with our parents is still important and can provide many treasured memories.

During quality time together, be positive and give your child the opportunity to relax. Have fun together. Allow yourself to be a little vulnerable. For example, share challenging experiences you had as a child. This will help your child to understand that you are not perfect, but that you are willing to learn, grow and change. Quality time is most certainly not the time to be reprimanding your child about any behaviour that you disapprove of.

Encourage your child to share their interests, activities, favourite foods and experiences with you and do the same. Use as many opportunities as possible to get to know your child, and give your child the opportunity to get to know you.

Responsibilities

It is the right of our children to be given responsibilities. The United Nations convention states that it is a child's right to participate in society.

No child is too young to be given responsibilities. What is critical is that the responsibilities are age appropriate. When we do not give our children appropriate responsibilities, we rob them of opportunities to become creative, inventive and self-reliant.

Education is not just about going to school and learning how to read and write. A rounded education will include the development of a sense of responsibility for oneself as well as towards others. A child needs to know, from a young age how to take responsibility for themselves and their actions. The home is the place to teach such principles, for example, looking after younger siblings is one way our children can learn to be responsible for others.

Coordination, planning, strategic thinking, time-management and cooperation are some of the essential skills that develop when our children are given responsibilities.

What to do:

1-3 years old
Give your child little jobs around the house, for example, tidying up shoes, folding socks etc. with supervision, as necessary.

4-6 years old
Get your child to help with household routines, for example, setting the table or preparing a cold breakfast. Children in this age group are often inconsistent in their use of logic and wish to appear competent. Hence safety rules in particular need to be carefully explained with a clear description of what constitutes safe behaviour. Children of this age group need careful supervision.

7-11 years old
Give your child simple tasks requiring more independence such as carrying the shopping from the car, washing up dishes, cleaning up their room etc. Encourage your child to work cooperatively with other members of the family. Warning: Physical development may outstrip mental or emotional maturity and children may express a desire to practice new skills without adult supervision, before they are mentally and emotionally capable of doing so.

12 -16 years old
At this age, young people can be given tasks such as small food shopping for the family, vacuuming, cooking part of the family's meal etc. Being active at school and in the community and taking part in voluntary work should be encouraged. The significance of peer influence can mean that adolescents may prefer to be socialising with their friends rather than carrying out their family responsibilities. Hence consistent expectations and consequences for not being responsible are key.

Continue to celebrate your child's strengths and develop their self-esteem by finding out what responsibilities they have taken on at school and in the community. Be sure to notice what responsibilities your child may have chosen to take on at home without being asked.

S

Solution Building Tools

We are often so protective of our children, to the extent that we want to solve all of their problems. However, we need to be reminded that it is better to prepare them to solve their own problems and deal with challenges but with support from us.

This solution building tool will help our children to tackle some of the challenges they will meet on their life's journey, for example, being bullied or having to deal with loss. It will help them to stop, think and be reflective before responding to the situation. This will help them to be more rational and less reactive. It is a practical tool that is to be used once our children are calm.

We need to teach our children strategies to bring down their emotional temperature, especially if they are angry about the issue to be resolved.

What to do:

Help your child to identify the challenge, for example, ask why is it a challenge.

Ask your child how they would like the outcome to look and feel. For example, their response might be, "so that I am not always so nervous."

Encourage your child to think of a number of approaches which could be used to obtain the desired outcome.

Support your child in examining the positives and negatives of using each of their suggested approaches and look at the long and short term consequences. You may need to suggest one or two additional approaches.

Allow your child, with support, to decide on the approach which they think will be the most effective and appropriate. The only exception to this should be where there is an implication for the health and safety of your child or others involved. In this case, it may be necessary for you to take the lead and do something which they might not agree with.

Once the decision has been made, support your child in planning the details.

Support your child in following through on the decision and evaluate it afterwards. If the approach used was unsuccessful, look at the other alternatives and try another.

Time for You

As adults we need time for ourselves for raising our children can be very demanding and time consuming. In order to be able to parent well, we must take time out for ourselves. This can be done even when we are at home with our children. We need to teach them how to give us space when we need it for appropriate periods of time. For example, we can explain to a four year old that we want to sit on the settee and have a drink, without interruption for ten minutes. Hence, we need them to play independently for the next few minutes. This is another way of modelling self-care.

We must remember teachers have thirty odd children in their classes and each child has their own set of needs. In this context children have to learn to wait their turn for attention. We must help our children to become self-disciplined, as well as to be able to negotiate in relation to their needs and the needs of others at an early age. In learning respect for our time and space, our children will learn to expect the same for themselves and respect that need in teachers and other people in the community.

What to do:

Call your child by name.

Look your child in the eyes.

Tell your child that you need to rest or do something for the amount of time you require. (You can buy an egg timer for a young child so that they can easily see when the time is up.)

Ask your child to explain what you have said.

Negotiate with your child what they need to do while you are resting.

Ask the child to repeat what you both agreed in order to avoid misunderstanding.

Hug your child and say, 'Thank you for allowing me some personal time.

Take the time you agreed. In so doing you are being consistent, respectful and honest with your child. This is modelling reliability and integrity.

If your child was obedient, hug them and say, "Thank you for allowing me to rest."

If on occasion you take more time than agreed, apologise, and discuss your reasons with your child.

Ensure the time is age appropriate and the activities for young children are safe. Very young children should be in the same room with you and can play with their toys for ten minutes.

Unity is Strength

A strong family unit is one that acknowledges the needs, views and strengths of all the members. Decisions are made by discussions based on ground rules that ensure mutual respect. Share decisions and ensure that leadership and social skills are developed in our children.

In a family discussion, there must be leadership, but everyone must be respected and given the opportunity to be involved.

The discussions could be about a family dinner, a trip to the park, who does what chores, an entertainment or religious devotion. Remember that games, such as sports or board games, encourage a healthy attitude toward competition and cooperation and allow you to discuss more difficult feelings such as jealousy. You might decide as a family to attend museums and cultural events, or allow the children to choose in turn.

As a result of being involved in decision-making our children are more likely to be better able to adopt a more supportive and co-operative approach to decision-making in other contexts, such as doing group work at school.

What to do:

Conducting a family discussion

Before the Family Discussion:
. Give notice, reason and time for the discussion.

. Emphasize the importance of punctuality.

At the Family Discussion:
· Start with welcoming and thanking everyone for attending.

· Agree on who will chair the discussion (initially parents or an older child may need to model good practice).

· Agree the ground rules. For example one person speaks at a time or family members can disagree but cannot insult each other.

· Explore the issue - give everyone the opportunity to have a say.

· Summarise the discussion and final decisions or actions.

· Decide on the next steps according to the decision of the family.

· Delegate responsibilities - who will take responsibility for finding the price of tickets, for example.

· Monitor progress and ensure that everyone follows through on whatever was agreed

· Review the outcome - If the approach was unsuccessful, be positive and learn from what did not go according to plan. Encourage everyone to be honest.

Visions for the Future

There will generally be conflicting needs and priorities in every family. However, the most successful families know how to handle disagreements and differing priorities in a creative and empowering way. Challenges can be seen as a force to create new ideas and improve the family for the future.

Successful families make sure that challenges are aired, understood and resolved as far as is possible. It may mean agreeing to differ, respecting each other's individuality and uniqueness. It may also mean that individuals in the family have to delay having their needs met in the short term, in order to ensure stability and success for the family in the long term. To do this, families need to get together regularly to talk through dreams, plans and goals. Families also need to share new information, ask for help and support as necessary, air concerns and challenges and create visions for the future.

What to do:

Help your child to set goals for one week, six months, one year, or two years depending on their age. For example your child might like to be good at swimming or at spelling words. Talk about what is involved in becoming good at spelling. With your child, find out more from teachers or books about the best ways to learn how to spell. In relation to swimming, you could do some research together on the internet, or go to the library and borrow DVDs on becoming a champion swimmer. Watch the DVD together and talk about it.

Work out a plan in order to achieve the goals set. Help your child to be ambitious but also realistic. For example ten new spellings a week could be a hard target for a small child but an appropriate target for an older child. Going swimming three times a week, having the right diet, and getting enough rest would be important elements of a plan for a child to become a champion swimmer.

Celebrate all progress and successes.

Review the plan and assess levels of progress and achievements against the targets.

Always praise new interests in learning and positive efforts, even when they may not go as planned.

W

Wisdom Equals Emotional Literacy

If we don't acknowledge our emotions, especially anger and grief, our unresolved emotions will cause us to behave irresponsibly or have an adverse effect on our health. For example, suppressed grief has been found to have a strong link to cancer. I once counselled a man who suffered from a stroke because his family discouraged him from crying over the death of his father. At our opening session, after we discussed this, he wept openly, which startled me because I had never heard a grown man weep with such intensity before.

It is important to help our children to recognise their emotions and to soar like eagles by managing their emotional world. It is also important that we allow our children to feel what they are feeling and to express their feelings in some way. In our society, anger is often discouraged in girls and sadness is discouraged in boys. This is not helpful. An emotional vocabulary is as important as an academic one.

It is okay to be angry or sad, it is how these emotions are managed that is more important. Our emotions are a choice and should never be allowed to rule us. Hurting others when we are hurt resolves nothing, it makes matters worse.

Having feelings is part of our humanity and our feelings need to be honoured. How we express our emotions will be influenced by our individuality and our cultural heritage.

What to do:

Make it a habit to talk openly about the whole range of your feelings with your child. For example, let it show when you are excited and talk about your excitement.

Managing angry feelings is often challenging. When we are angry it is important to say so and explain why. By stating clearly that we are angry, we are taking ownership of our feelings and modelling appropriate anger management.

When feeling overwhelmed, take a deep breath and count to ten inside. Tell your child you are angry about their behaviour or attitude and you will discuss it later. This could mean sending the child to another room or area. Be careful to separate the child from the behaviour.

When you are ready, deal with what has just happened in a fair way. This means:

> · Being prepared to listen to your child's point of view. This will help build positive self-esteem in your child by demonstrating that the child is worthy of respect. (i.e. worth listening to). It will also develop your child's confidence to speak up.
>
> · Not interrupting and asking whether they have finished.
>
> · Checking that you have really understood.
>
> · Explaining why the behaviour was unacceptable.
>
> · Explaining what will happen next and why.

Always explain to your child when you are feeling sad and don't be afraid to allow them to see you crying, but make a careful judgement about whether your child is mature enough to be able to handle seeing you deeply distraught. This is especially important for fathers.

X

RelaX and Let Go

Letting go of our children can be very difficult. For years, they are dependent upon us for so many things then suddenly they need their independence and we must step back so that they can go forward. This can be especially challenging when we are raising children in single parent households. Too often, we want to live our unfulfilled dreams through them rather than allowing them to have their own aspirations. Our children's achievements often give us a sense of personal achievement and purpose. To avoid this, we need to continue to fulfil our own ambitions for ourselves within the framework of family responsibilities.

Our personal and professional development should not stop because we are parents. We should make time and create opportunities to grow alongside our children by studying in formal contexts and at home.

By nurturing our own growth, we will find strength when our children become teenagers, begin to form other close relationships and assert their independence. Once we have maintained a strong sense of self, when they are ready to leave home, we will be able to celebrate and help them to make the transition, even though it may be painful to experience them leaving.

What to do:

Plan for your personal and professional development. For example, if you want to take a degree once your child is older, research where and what you could study well in advance.

On a regular basis, arrange for a reliable, experienced and trustworthy person to look after your child so that you can have personal time alone with your partner or with friends. Ensure that you explain all arrangements fully to your child.

Try to be a member of at least one group and become actively involved.

Regularly browse the personal development section of your local bookshop for relevant topics. Use the internet as a source of information.

Develop close relationships with at least one group of friends who will help you grow and develop. Spend time with them at least once a month.

Develop your hobbies and interests and share them with your child.

Explore career guidance and coaching if you are finding it difficult to decide on a career or to get motivated.

Seek counselling if you know that unresolved issues are preventing you from moving forward.

Youthfulness

To stay youthful and healthy we need to pay close attention to our diets. Nutrition greatly affects the state of our minds and bodies. We are what we eat. How well we parent is likely to be greatly affected by the state of our health.

Our children become what we feed them. It is important that they are fed a tasty, enjoyable, healthy and balanced diet. In a balanced diet, the meal should include foods from the basic food groups. The body must be fed but not just by filling the stomach with anything. The kinds of food we eat are very important.

Young children need a lot of protein to develop as well as vitamins and minerals for protection against diseases. More active children need extra carbohydrate for energy.

In addition, we need to take some form of regular exercise in order to build strength, stamina and flexibility. This might include aerobics class, running, basketball or dance classes.

Consuming sufficient water is critical to our general health since our bodies are over 70% water. Many schools now encourage pupils to carry a bottle of water to class and drink when they are thirsty. This greatly aids concentration.

What to do:

Feed your child on a daily basis from the basic food groups which are **Proteins, Carbohydrates, Fats, Oils, Vitamins, Minerals and Fibres**

Proteins
Protein is required to build and repair all tissues, produce antibodies, fight infection, supply energy and form the basis for blood and hormones. Some healthy sources of protein are soya milk, yogurt, cheese, poultry, fish, beans, pulses, tofu and nuts.

Carbohydrates
Carbohydrates are required to supply energy and to help the body to use other nutrients. Some good sources of carbohydrate are bread, cereal, rice, sweet potatoes and yam.

Fats, Oils
Fats and oils supply food energy. Essential fatty acids provide for healthy skin and protect delicate organs. Some good sources are olive oil, corn oil, hemp oil, oily fish and avocados.

Vitamins and Minerals
Vitamins and minerals keep the skin and nervous system healthy, help convert sugars and starchy foods to energy and heat, help resist diseases, promote healing, as well as the absorption of calcium to make bones stronger. Healthy sources of vitamins include guavas, mangoes, peas, carrots, leafy vegetables, spinach, cabbage, bananas, apples and melon. Healthy sources of minerals include turnips, parsley, green banana and kelp.

Fibres
Fibre helps to keep the bowels working regularly and provides us with some nutrients. Healthy sources include the following: wholegrain rice, beans, pulses, dates, figs, prunes, lentils, cabbage, kale and oats. In cases where bowel movements are infrequent (i.e. the person is constipated) the herb Cascara Sagrada is an excellent remedy. Seek the advice of a herbalist for dosage.

Zero Tolerance For Abuse

Sexual and physical abuse can happen under our noses. We need to **zoom** right in on what our children are saying and doing. Reluctance to visit someone could be more significant than we think. The abuser could be the person we most trusted to look after our children. Let us be very aware and vigilant.

Sometimes we emotionally abuse our children by constantly shouting, criticising or neglecting them in favour of our own pursuits and interests. Sometimes, we smack our children believing it to be for their own good, since that was our own childhood experience, hence not realising the damage and hurt we are causing.

It is important that we are able to recognise the symptoms of physical and emotional abuse. As the symptoms often overlap with each other and other medical conditions, we must always check with our doctor to be sure. If there is abuse, we must talk sensitively with our children and seek professional support.

There is contact information for organisations who may be able to help at the back of this book.

What to do:

How to recognise Mental Abuse and Emotional Abuse

There are likely to be signs of:
· depression, emotional withdrawal, social isolation, sleep disorders, self-mutilating behaviours, extremely low self esteem, excessive anxiety, addictions to drugs such as alcohol, suicidal tendencies, attention-seeking behaviours, telling lies, inability to have fun, tantrums past the age when this is part of normal development, speech disorders e.g. stammering, inability to play and indiscriminate displays of affection.

How to recognise Sexual abuse

There are likely to be signs of:
· bruises or scratches inconsistent with accidental injury, difficulty in walking or sitting, pain or itching in the genital area, torn, stained or bloody underclothes, bed-wetting, sleep disturbances, loss of appetite, hints of sexual activity through words, play, drawing etc, use of sexually explicit language, poor self-esteem, withdrawal or isolating self from other children.

How to recognise Physical abuse

There are likely to be signs of:
· facial bruising, hand or finger marks or pressure bruising, bite marks, burns (particularly cigarette burns), scalds, unexpected fractures, lacerations or abrasions, shying away from physical contact, withdrawn or aggressive behaviour or inexplicable changes in behaviour.

Parenting Acrostic Poem

P   Praising our precious children

A   Adoring and appreciating our children, our special gifts from God

R   Relishing the responsibilities of parenting

E   Empowering ourselves to be the best parents we can be

N   Nurturing ourselves and our children

T   Teaching through modelling

I   Inspiring through our words and actions

N   Negotiating lovingly

G   Giving love unconditionally

Other Publications by Karlene Rickard:

1. A Guide To African Caribbean Foods From A to Z
2. A Child's Guide To Tropical Foods

Helpful Organisations

www.parenting-forum.org

Parenting UK
431 Highgate Studios
53-79 Highgate Road
London NW5 1TL
Tel:020 7284 8370
www.parenting-forum.org.uk

www.relate.org.uk

www.nspcc.org.uk
(National Society for the
Prevention of Cruelty to
Children)

www.bbc.co.uk/parenting/tv_and
_radio/childline

www.tsa.uk.com (Trust for the
Study of Adolescence)

NSPCC Free 24 Child
protection Helpline 0808 800
500 (UK)

Childline Number 0800 1111
(UK), www.childline.org.uk

http://step-by-step.org.uk/

One Parent Families
Addresses issues and problems
facing
Single parents familie

Helpline: 0800 018 5026

www.oneparentfamilies.org.uk

National Family and Parenting
Institute (NFPI) – UK

Offers support for people
bringing up children
Tel: 020 7424 3460
www.nfpi.org.uk

For Parents for Parents
Provides information and advice
to parents
www.forparentsbyparnts.co.uk

Dad' Haven Advice and
information for Dad's www.dads-
haven.co.uk

Home-Start
For parents finding it hard to
cope
With children under five
Freephone: 0800 686 368
www.home-start.org.uk

Underpinning The A to Z of Parenting is a common set of
principles identified by the "Every Child Matters" agenda.

Bibliography

Beardshaw, Tom. Hordern, Guy & Tufnell, Christine (2000) *Single Parents in focus*, Care For the Family.

Bernard Van Leer Foundation (February 2001) *Early Childhood Matters: Fathers matter too*, Bernard Van Leer Foundation.

Biddulph, Steve (1998) *Raising Boys*, Thorsons.

Carson, Ben (1996) Gifted Hands, Zondervan publishing house.

Chalke, Steve (1997) *How to Succeed As A Parent*, Hodder & Stoughton.

Cousin, Pierre Jean (2001) *Food Is Medicine*, Duncan Baird Publishers.

Dobson, DR James (1970) *The new dare to discipline*, Tyndale House Publishers.

Dwivedi, Kedar Nath (1997) *Enhancing Parenting Skills*, WILEY.

Faber, Adele & Mazlish, Elaine (2001) *"How to Talk So Kids will Listen & Listen so Kids Will Talk"*, Piccadilly Press Ltd.

Family Links (1994) The Nurturing Programme, Adaptation prepared by Mountford, Annette & Hunt, Candida, Family Developing Resources Inc.

Freeman, Becky (2003) Lifelines: *Survival Tips For Parents Of Preschoolers*, TYNDALE.

Goleman, Daniel (1996) *Emotional Intelligence*, Bloomsbury.

Hartley-Brewer, Elizabeth (1994) *Positive Parenting: Raising Children with Self- esteem*, Mandarin Paperbacks.

Hartley-Brewer, Elizabeth (2000) *Self- Esteem For Boys*, Vermilion. Jamaica Coalition on the Rights of the child (June 2000) Rights and Responsibilities, (JCRC).

Henry, Ava & Williams, Michael (1999) Black Scientists and Inventors Book 1, BIS Publications LTD.

Newham Area Child Protection Committee *The Safe Parenting Handbook*, SureStart Newham.

Rogers, Carl (1978) Carl Rogers on Person Power, Constable.

Ruttle, Kate & Young Annemarie (2005) *Helping Your Child to Read*, Oxford University Press.

Rickard, Karlene (2000), *A Guide to African Caribbean Foods From A to Z*, BIS Publications, London.

Rickard, Karlene (2003), *A Child's Guide to Tropical Foods*, BIS Publications, London

Simon, David (2004) *How to Unlock Your Child's Genius*) Ebony Books. London.

The A to Z of Parenting ensures Every Child Matters